S0-CGT-365

World Book, Inc.,
Tropical fish.
[2017]
33305241109705
ca   04/05/18

Tropical Fish

WORLD
BOOK

www.worldbook.com

World Book, Inc.
180 North LaSalle Street
Suite 900
Chicago, Illinois 60601
USA

© 2018 World Book, Inc. All rights reserved. This book may not be reproduced in whole or in part in any form without prior written permission from the publisher.

WORLD BOOK and the GLOBE DEVICE are registered trademarks or trademarks of World Book, Inc.

For information about other World Book publications, visit our website at **www.worldbook.com** or call **1-800-WORLDBK (967-5325)**.

For information about sales to schools and libraries, call **1-800-975-3250 (United States); 1-800-837-5365 (Canada)**.

Library of Congress Cataloging-in-Publication Data for this volume has been applied for.

World Book's Learning Ladders
ISBN 978-0-7166-7945-5 (set, hc.)

Tropical Fish
ISBN 978-0-7166-7954-7 (hc.)

Also available as:
ISBN 978-0-7166-7964-6 (e-book)

Printed in China by Shenzhen Wing King Tong Paper Products Co, Ltd., Shenzhen, Guangdong
1st printing December 2017

Staff

Executive Committee
President: Jim O'Rourke
Vice President and Editor in Chief: Paul A. Kobasa
Vice President, Finance: Donald D. Keller
Vice President, Marketing: Jean Lin
Vice President, International Sales: Maksim Rutenberg
Vice President, Technology: Jason Dole
Director, Human Resources: Bev Ecker

Editorial
Director, New Print Publishing: Tom Evans
Senior Editor, New Print Publishing: Shawn Brennan
Writer: Kendra Muntz
Director, Digital Product Content Development: Emily Kline
Manager, Indexing Services: David Pofelski
Manager, Contracts & Compliance (Rights & Permissions): Loranne K. Shields
Librarian: S. Thomas Richardson

Digital
Director, Digital Product Development: Erika Meller
Digital Product Manager: Jonathan Wills

Graphics and Design
Senior Art Director: Tom Evans
Coordinator, Design Development and Production: Brenda Tropinski
Senior Visual Communications Designer: Melanie J. Bender
Media Researcher: Rosalia Bledsoe

Manufacturing/Pre-Press
Manufacturing Manager: Anne Fritzinger
Proofreader: Nathalie Strassheim

Photographic credits: Cover: © Richard Whitcombe, Shutterstock; Architect of the Capitol: 21; © Dreamstime: 22; © Wild Horizons/UIG/Getty Images: 8; © iStockphoto: 20; © Shutterstock: 5, 6, 11, 12, 14, 17, 18, 26, 27.

Illustrators: WORLD BOOK illustrations by Quadrum Ltd

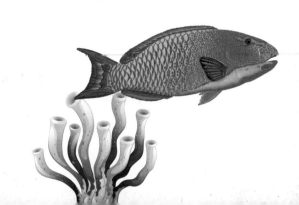

What's inside?

This book tells you about some beautiful and interesting fish that live in tropical waters around the world. Some fish are tiny, others are huge, but they all share a home in Earth's ocean.

# The tropics

Many different kinds of fish live in the sea in parts of the world called the tropics. The tropics are a warm area near the equator. The equator is an imaginary line that goes around the middle of Earth. There are rain forests on the land and coral reefs in the ocean in the tropics. The fish that live in the tropics are called tropical fish.

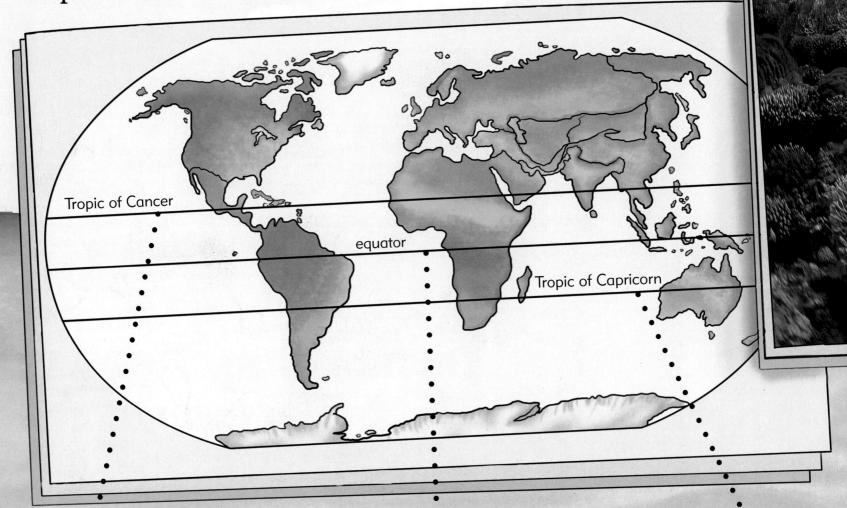

Tropic of Cancer

equator

Tropic of Capricorn

The northern edge of the tropics is an imaginary line called the **Tropic of Cancer.**

The **equator** divides Earth in half.

The southern edge of the tropics is an imaginary line called the **Tropic of Capricorn.**

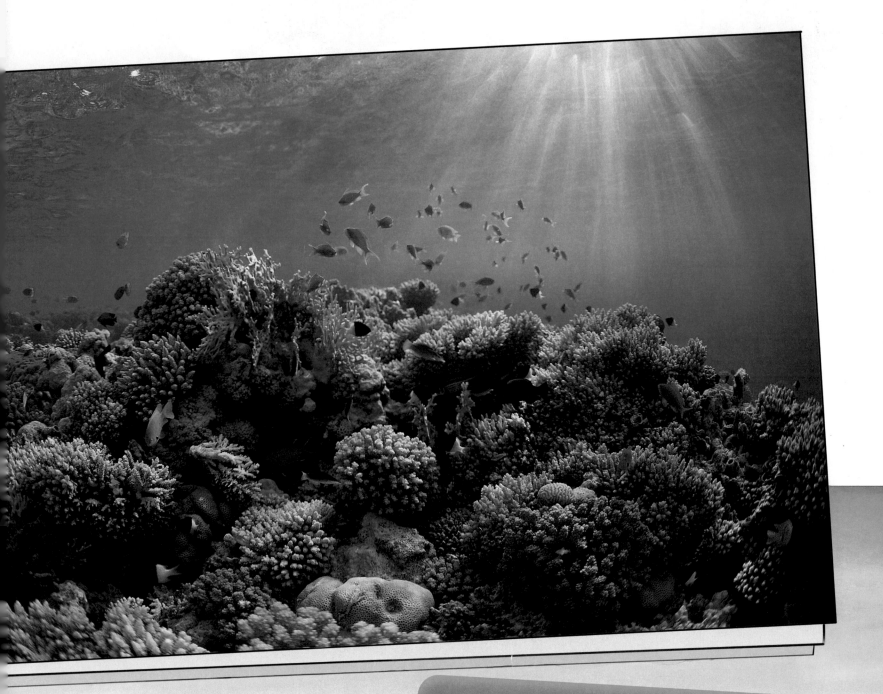

Many fish and other animals in the tropics live in coral reefs. These reefs are like underwater cities where fish swim among the **coral** (rocky structures formed by millions of tiny animals). Coral grows in many colors, shapes, and sizes.

It's a fact!

Some coral reefs are dying because the sea water is getting warmer. We can help protect the reefs by not damaging the air, water, and land around us.

Clownfish

Colorful clownfish live around sea anemones *(uh NEHM uh neez)* in coral reefs. A sea anemone is a kind of sea animal that looks like a plant. Clownfish are found in the warm waters of the Pacific and Indian oceans. The largest clownfish grow from 4 to 6 1/2 inches (10 to 17 centimeters) long.

Clownfish have a bright orange body with white **stripes** outlined in black.

Clownfish are partners with **sea anemones**. The anemone uses its feelers to sting other animals. But the feelers do not hurt the clownfish. Staying close to the anemone protects the clownfish from being eaten by other sea animals. In return, the clownfish helps clean the anemone.

A coating on the clownfish's **skin** protects the fish from being stung by a sea anemone.

It's a fact!

Clownfish can scare away other animals by slamming their teeth together!

# Angelfish

There are many different kinds of angelfish swimming in the world's oceans. Angelfish that live in the tropics have bright body colors and patterns of scales. Scales make up the covering of the body of most fish.

The angelfish flicks its **tail fin** from side to side to quickly move through the water.

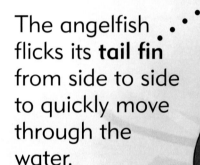

Some angelfish can get their food by helping larger reef fish stay clean. The angelfish eats things that have stuck to the bodies of larger fish. As the angelfish eat, they clean the larger fish.

The brightly colored **patterns** on its body help the angelfish to hide among the coral.

It's a fact!

As the angelfish swims, some people think its fins gently move like an angel's flapping wings. That's one idea of how the angelfish got its name!

Angelfish have a thin, **oval body** to help them glide through the water.

Moray eel

The moray eel looks like a snake but swims like a fish! Its long, thin body slithers in, out, above, and below the coral reef's many shapes. Moray eels hide in the reef's cracks and holes. They quickly swim out to catch passing fish.

A moray eel has one **fin** that runs along the top of its body.

The moray eel has a **slippery body** to help it slide in and out of jagged cracks in the coral.

It's a fact!

Be careful! If you see a moray eel in the water, don't touch it! Moray eels may attack a swimmer if they get scared.

Watch out for eels!

The **spotted body** pattern helps the eel to blend into the coral.

When the eel rests at the bottom of the reef, some types of **shrimp** will help the eel keep clean. These cleaner shrimp crawl over the eel, eating things that have stuck to it.

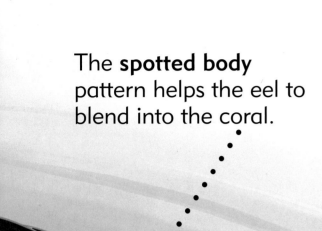

The eel has **sharp teeth** and powerful **jaws** that it uses to catch fish to eat.

The large, **flat tail** helps push the eel through the water.

The moray eel opens and closes its **mouth** to breathe.

Porcupinefish

The porcupinefish can "puff up" like a balloon! When an enemy scares the porcupinefish, it fills its stomach with water. Then, the fish's body puffs up and sharp spikes stick out of it. An enemy changes its mind about eating this fish!

The fish can **puff up** to about two times its normal size!

The porcupinefish's body gives off a poison when the fish is frightened. This poison can hurt other fish and people, too.

Strong, sharp **spines** cover the porcupinefish's body. The spines usually lie flat against its body when the fish is calm.

The porcupinefish looks very gentle when it is not puffed up!

Unlike most fish, the porcupinefish can blink and close its **eyes**.

This **crab** is about to become dinner for the porcupinefish! The fish also eats sea urchins and other animals with hard shells.

Two large **teeth**, one upper and one lower, stick out like a beak.

It's a fact!

Porcupinefish are named after porcupines because the fish's sharp spines look like stiff porcupine quills. Both animals stick their spikes out to protect themselves from enemies.

Trumpetfish

Trumpetfish are very long and skinny coral reef fish. Their body is usually a reddish color with dark spots. Trumpetfish can change their body coloring to green, yellow, blue, or purple to match the color of nearby coral. This coloring helps to hide the fish among the tall corals.

The trumpetfish likes to play tricks on other fish! It can hold its body straight up and down to blend in with tall coral. It will stay very still until it sees a passing fish, and then quickly swim out and suck the fish into its mouth!

The trumpetfish swims very slowly using its **back fin** and **tail fin.**

The trumpetfish is named after the musical instrument because of its **long, thin body.** The fish can grow up to 6 feet (1.8 meters) long.

A **tube-shaped mouth** sucks up small fish like a vacuum cleaner sucks up dirt.

Seven pairs of **gills** help the fish breathe underwater.

It's a fact!

Like its seahorse relative, the mother trumpetfish gives her eggs to a father trumpetfish. He keeps them in a special pouch on his body until they are ready to hatch.

Frogfish

The frogfish is playing hide and seek among the coral! The frogfish is very good at hiding in the reef. Small, colorful bumps and lumps on its body look just like coral. Other fish cannot tell the difference, so they swim very close— only to be gobbled up by the frogfish!

A wiggly **growth** . . . . between the frogfish's eyes attracts other fish. The growth looks to them like food floating in the water.

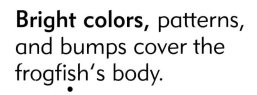 **Bright colors,** patterns, and bumps cover the frogfish's body.

The frogfish has a mouth that it can open really wide, just like a frog can!

It's a fact!

A frogfish can eat another fish twice its size! The frogfish uses its mouth to fold the fish and swallow it whole! It even has a stretchy stomach to hold those big meals!

The frogfish does not swim much. Instead, it uses its **fins** like legs to slowly crawl on the coral and the ocean floor.

Lionfish

Look! It's a fish that looks like a lion! Lionfish get their name from their long fins and pointy spines that look like a lion's big collar of fur—its mane. Stings from this fish's stiff, sharp spines can kill other fish and hurt people!

It's a fact!

Lionfish are also called turkeyfish or zebrafish because their coloring can make them look like all three of these animals!

Red lionfish have spread into parts of the sea where they did not live before. The lionfish can harm the animals and plants that are already there.

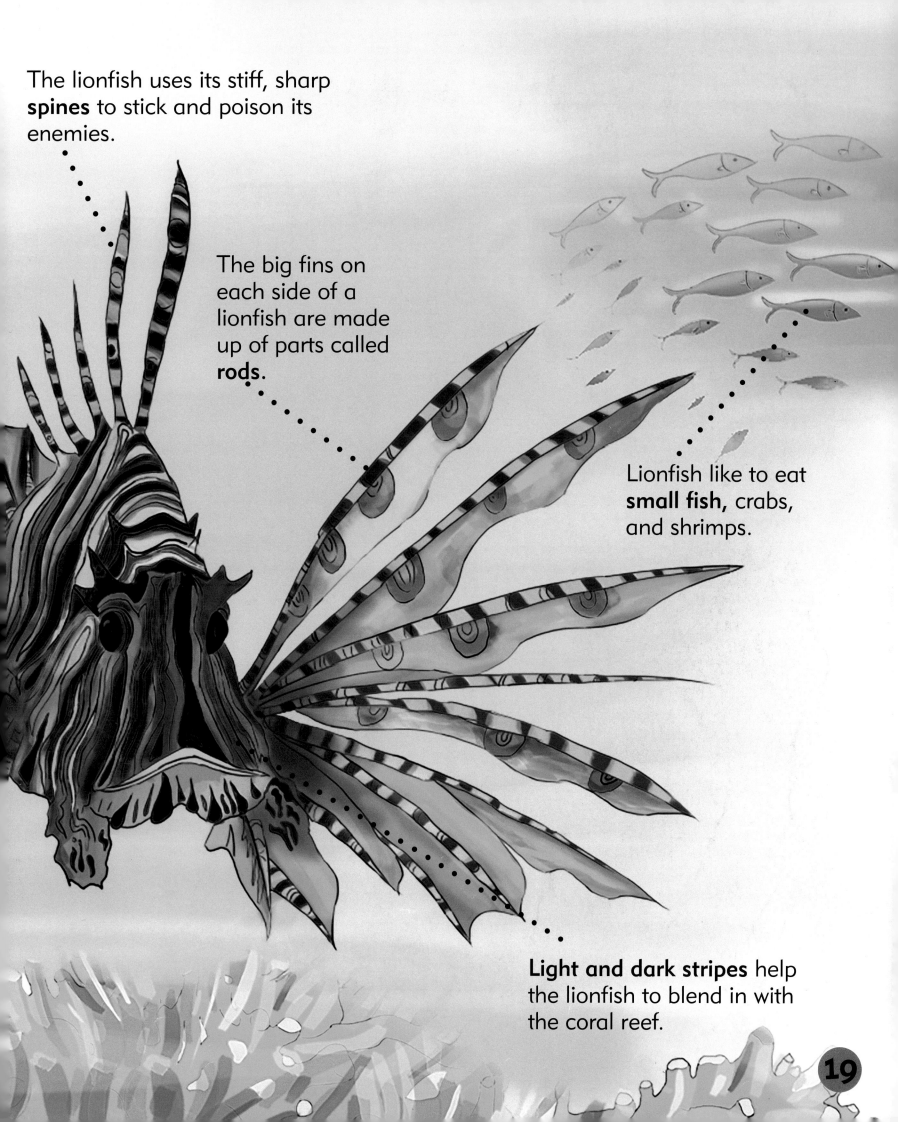

The lionfish uses its stiff, sharp **spines** to stick and poison its enemies.

The big fins on each side of a lionfish are made up of parts called **rods**.

Lionfish like to eat **small fish,** crabs, and shrimps.

Light and dark stripes help the lionfish to blend in with the coral reef.

Flounder

Flounders live on the sandy and muddy bottoms of bays and along the shores of most seas. They lay flat against the sea floor. Other passing sea creatures—and people—do not see them!

Colored bands line the **fins**.

Flounders have markings on their body that help them blend in with the things around them. The side of the flounder facing up takes on the color of the bottom of the sea. The bottom side of the fish is nearly white. Can you find the flounder in the photo above?

A flounder has both **eyes** on one side of its body. Both eyes face upwards.

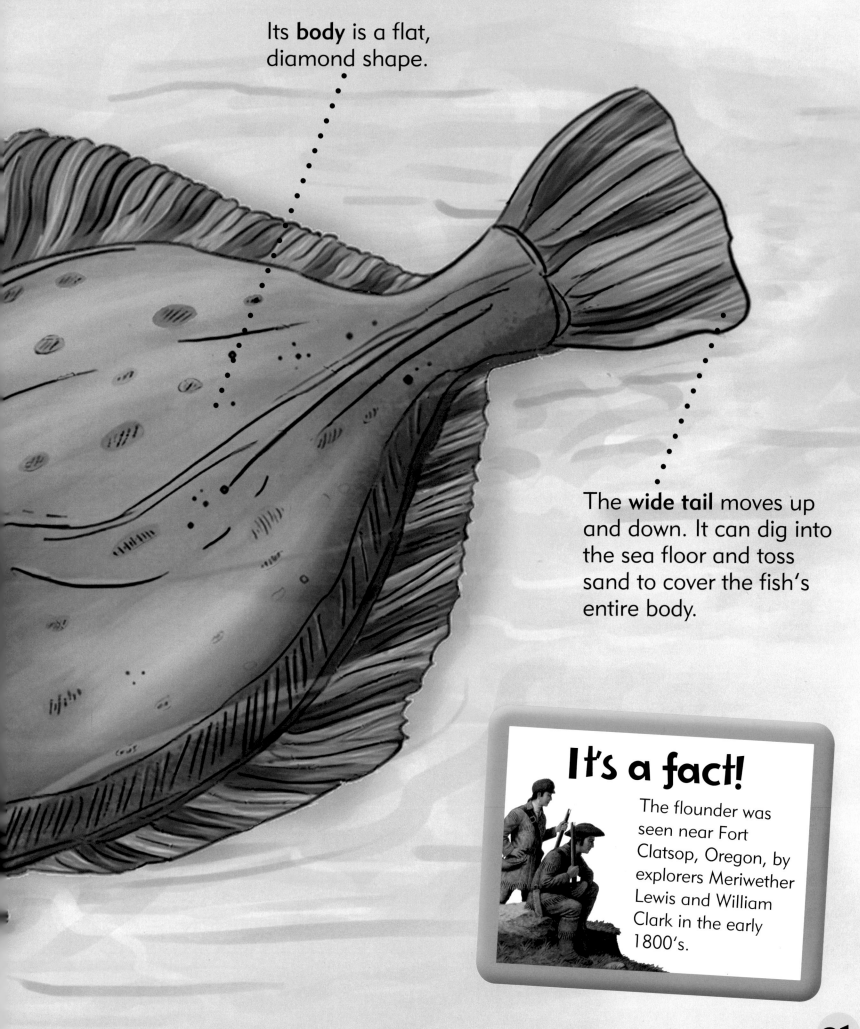

Its **body** is a flat, diamond shape.

The **wide tail** moves up and down. It can dig into the sea floor and toss sand to cover the fish's entire body.

It's a fact!

The flounder was seen near Fort Clatsop, Oregon, by explorers Meriwether Lewis and William Clark in the early 1800's.

Parrotfish

Parrotfish get their name from their unusual front teeth, which look like a parrot's beak. Parrotfish move around during the day and rest at night.

Large, thick **scales** cover the fish's body.

Many parrotfish make a sort of blanket for themselves at night. The blanket is see-through. The fish rests wrapped in its blanket until daylight when it swims off to explore the reef.

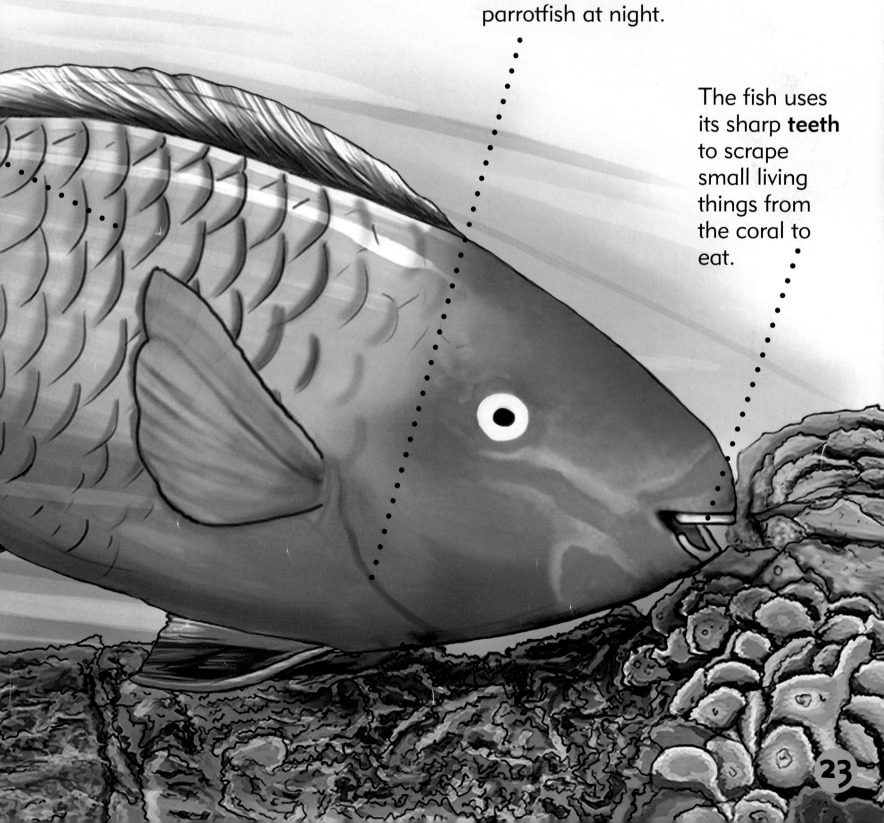

It's a fact!

Parrotfish are born a muddy brown color. As the fish grows up, it changes to a bright blue-green color.

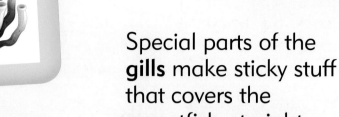

Special parts of the **gills** make sticky stuff that covers the parrotfish at night.

The fish uses its sharp **teeth** to scrape small living things from the coral to eat.

23

At the aquarium

You can see tropical fish up close at a type of museum called an aquarium *(uh KWAIR ee uhm)*. The fish are in large tanks. At the aquarium, fish and other sea creatures swim together, just as they do in the ocean.

24

Words you know

Here are some words that you read earlier in this book. Say them out loud, then try to find the things in the picture.

fin
scales
coral

gill
tail
teeth

Which fish have sharp spines?

25

Did you know?

The Great Barrier Reef near Australia is made up of more than 3,000 individual coral reefs.

Some fish live together in groups called schools. A school swims close together to keep safe from other sea animals that want to eat them.

People can wear special gear to dive into the water and see tropical fish living on coral reefs.

Fish are a type of vertebrate (an animal that has a backbone).

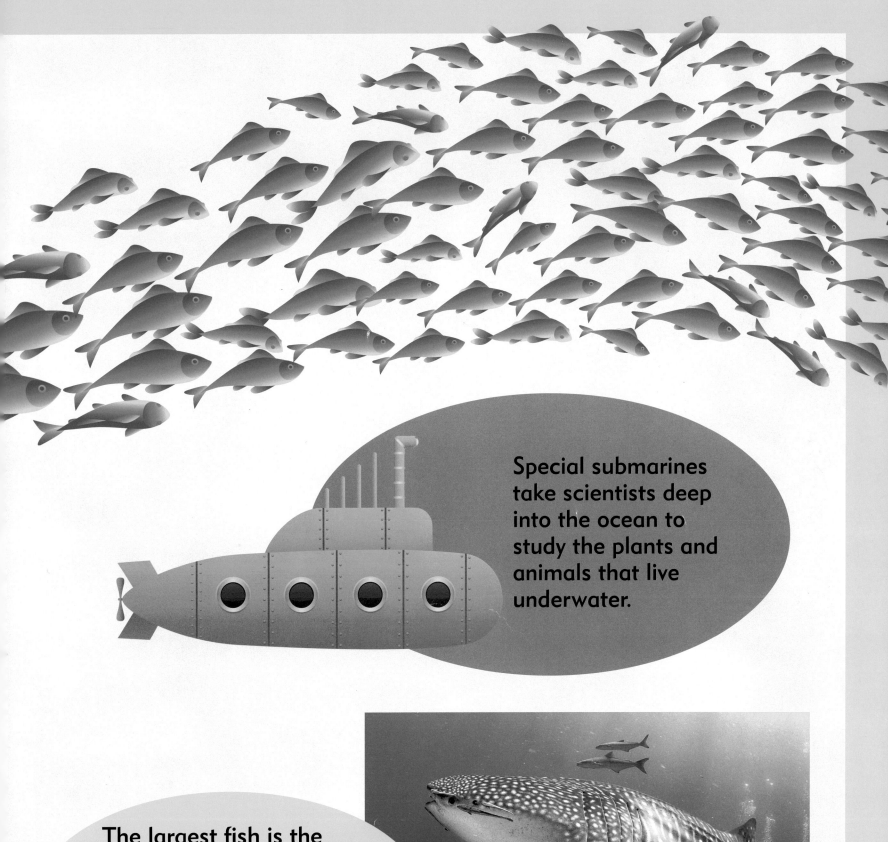

Special submarines take scientists deep into the ocean to study the plants and animals that live underwater.

The largest fish is the whale shark. It may weigh more than 15 short tons (14 metric tons). That's over twice as much as an African elephant!

Puzzles

Close-up!

We've zoomed in on parts of three different fish. Can you figure out which tropical fish you are looking at?

1

2

3

Double trouble!

These two pictures are not exactly the same. Can you find five things that are different in picture b?

a

b

Answers on page 32.

28

Match up!

Match each word on the left with its picture on the right.

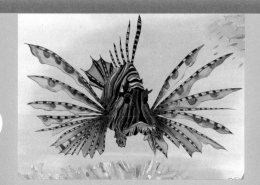
a

1. trumpetfish

b

2. moray eel

c

3. angelfish

d

4. clownfish

e

5. porcupinefish

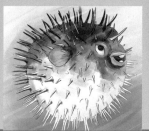
f

6. lionfish

Answers on page 32. **29**

True or false

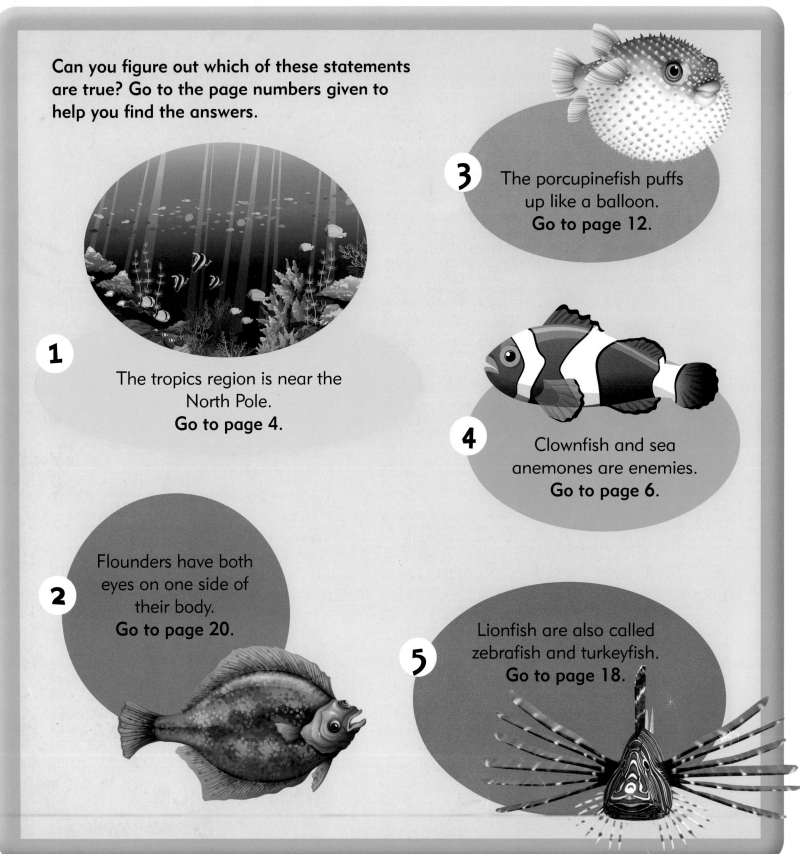

Can you figure out which of these statements are true? Go to the page numbers given to help you find the answers.

3 The porcupinefish puffs up like a balloon. **Go to page 12.**

1 The tropics region is near the North Pole. **Go to page 4.**

4 Clownfish and sea anemones are enemies. **Go to page 6.**

2 Flounders have both eyes on one side of their body. **Go to page 20.**

5 Lionfish are also called zebrafish and turkeyfish. **Go to page 18.**

Answers on page 32.

Find out more

Books

Fabulous Fishes by Susan Stockdale (Peachtree, 2012)
This boardbook looks at such fish as the clownfish, the lanternfish, and the hatchetfish. An afterword offers fascinating facts and a closer look at each fish.

National Geographic Little Kids First Big Book of the Ocean by Catherine D. Hughes (National Geographic Society, 2013)
This fully illustrated book introduces children to the wonders of underwater life.

Tropical Fish by Grace Hansen (ABDO, 2014)
Learn all about vibrant and beautiful tropical fish with this book illustrated with full-color photographs. Includes glossary, index, and table of contents.

What's It Like to Be a Fish? by Wendy Pfeffer (HarperCollins, 2015)
This picture book explains how a fish's body is perfectly designed for life in water. Simple, fun diagrams help explain concepts such as how fish use their gills to breathe underwater. It also includes an additional activity for kids to set up their own goldfish bowl.

Websites

Fish and Kids
https://fishandkids.msc.org/en
This site from the Marine Stewardship Council has pages for parents, teachers, and kids aimed at teaching children about the importance of marine sustainability. Includes fish-themed crafts, games, quizzes, facts, videos, activities, recipes, and classroom resources.

FishFAQ
http://www.nefsc.noaa.gov/faq/index.html
Woods Hole Science Aquarium answers many questions about fish, for example, "Do fish sleep?" and "What is chitin?"

Fun Fish Facts for Kids
http://easyscienceforkids.com/all-about-fish/
Learn about fish with this educational science website from Easy Science for Kids. Includes a quiz and printable worksheets.

National Geographic Kids
http://kids.nationalgeographic.com/animals/hubs/fish/
Learn about all kinds of fish on this website featuring photos, videos, and games.

Answers

Puzzles
from pages 28 and 29

Close-up!
1. angelfish
2. porcupinefish
3. flounder

Double trouble!
In picture b, the side fin on the small fish is missing, green leaves have been added in front of the coral in the lower right corner, the second rock in the lower right corner is missing, a starfish has been added, and the bigger fish is looking up.

Match up!
1. d   4. c
2. b   5. f
3. e   6. a

True or false
from page 30

1. false   4. false
2. true   5. true
3. true

Index